Anyone Can Teach ABCs

By LaTondra Moultrie

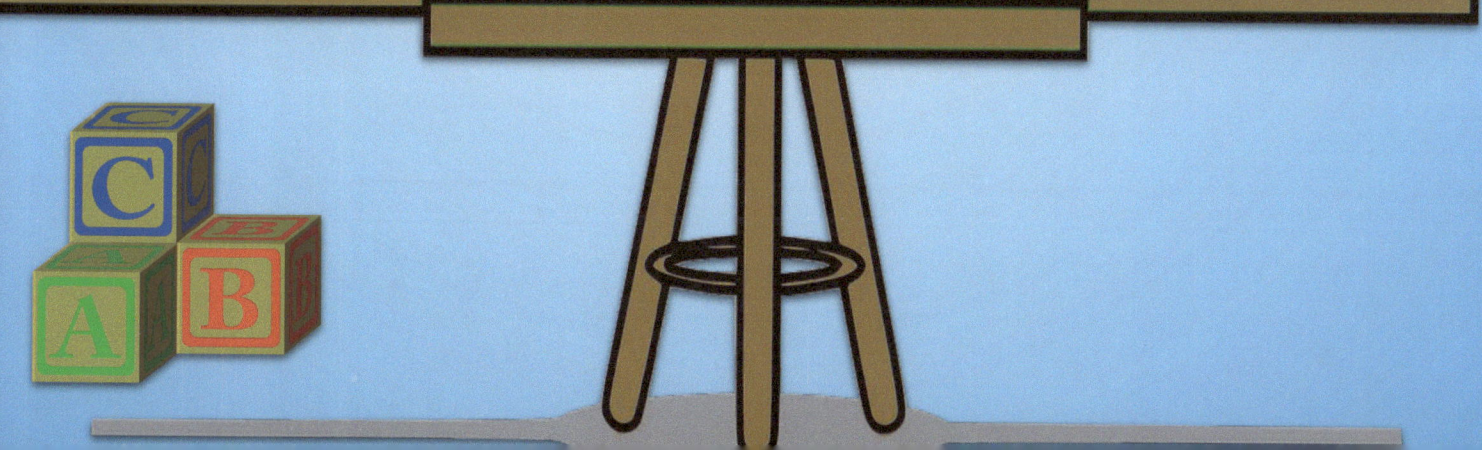

To Chalante' Te'Liyah, Aubrii and Averii

(c)2021, LaTondra Moultrie
All rights reserved

Anyone Can Teach is a Trademark of LaTondra Moultrie.
Trademarks may be registered in some jurisdictions.
All other trademarks are the property of their respective owners.

No claim to copyright is made for original U.S. Government Works.

No part of this document may be reproduced in any form or by any means, electronic, graphic, or mechanical, including but not limited to photocopying, information storage, and retrieval systems, without permission in writing from the publisher.

- Study with this book when your child is relaxed

- If your child loses interest, stop while having fun and try again later.

- Praise your child's success.

- There are 26 letters in the alphabet.
- Each alphabet has an uppercase letter and a lowercase letter.
- Practice the alphabet every day until your child recognizes each letter.
- Practice writing uppercase and lowercase letters each day.
- Introduce vowels, (a,e,i,o,u).
- Introduce consonants, (B,C,D,F,G,H,J,K,L,M,N,P,Q,R,S,T,V,W,X,Y,Z).

Aa Bb Cc Dd Ee
Ff Gg Hh Ii Jj Kk
Ll Mm Nn Oo Pp
Qq Rr Ss Tt Uu
Vv Ww Xx Yy Zz

Apple

Aa

Bb

Ball

Dd

Duck

Ee

Egg

Fish

Ff

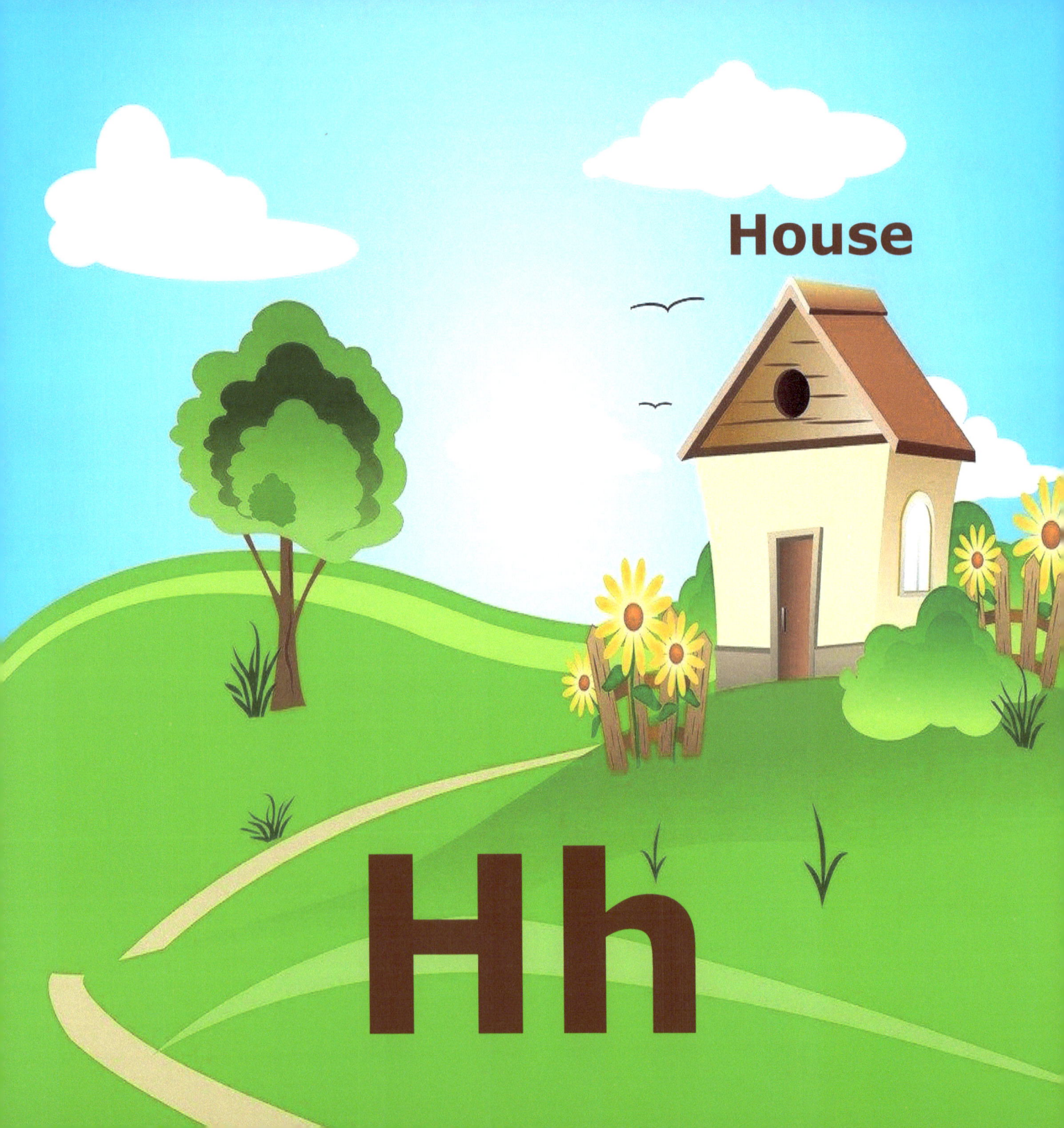

Ii

Igloo

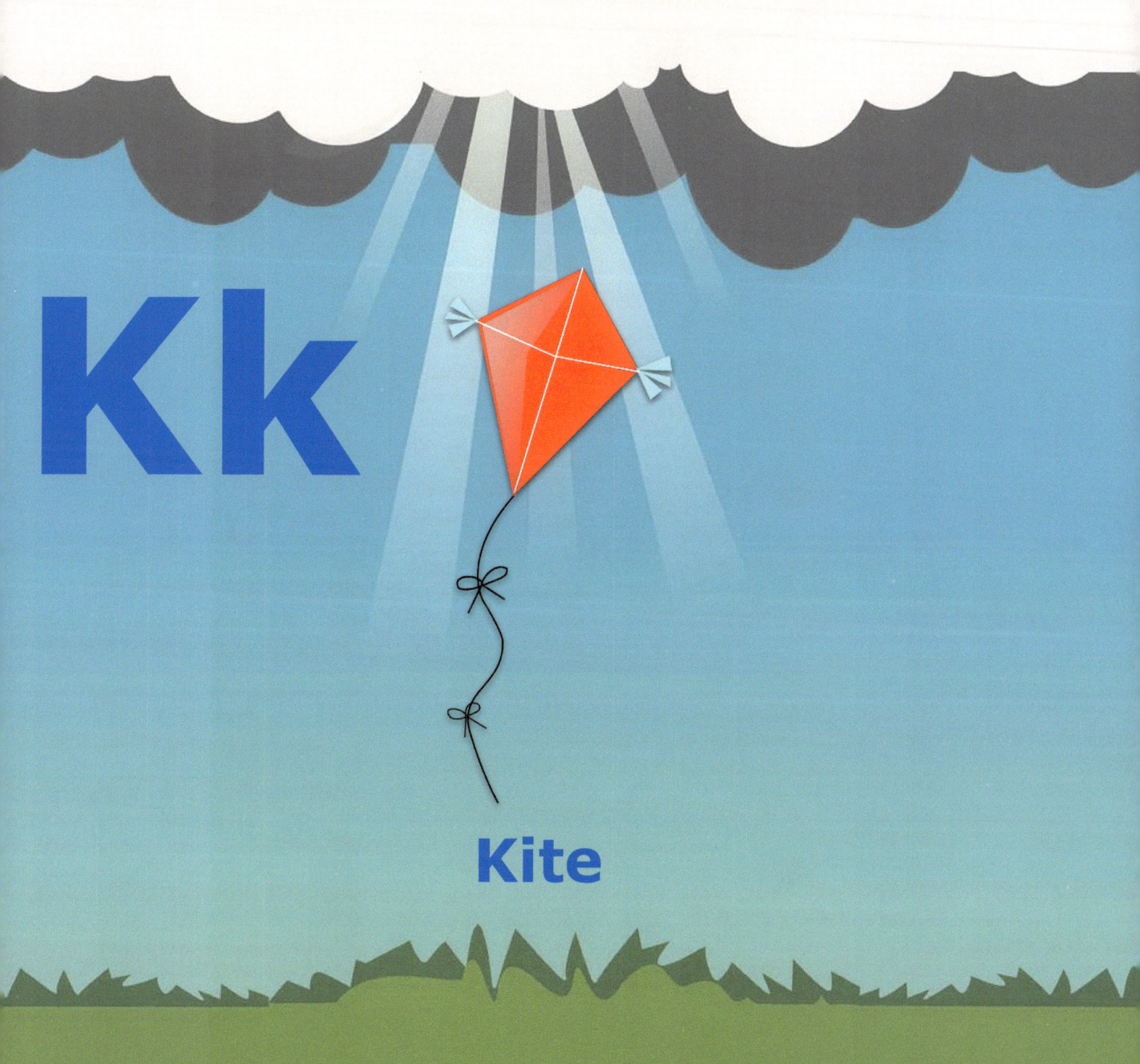

Nn

Necklace

Qq

Quilt

Rr

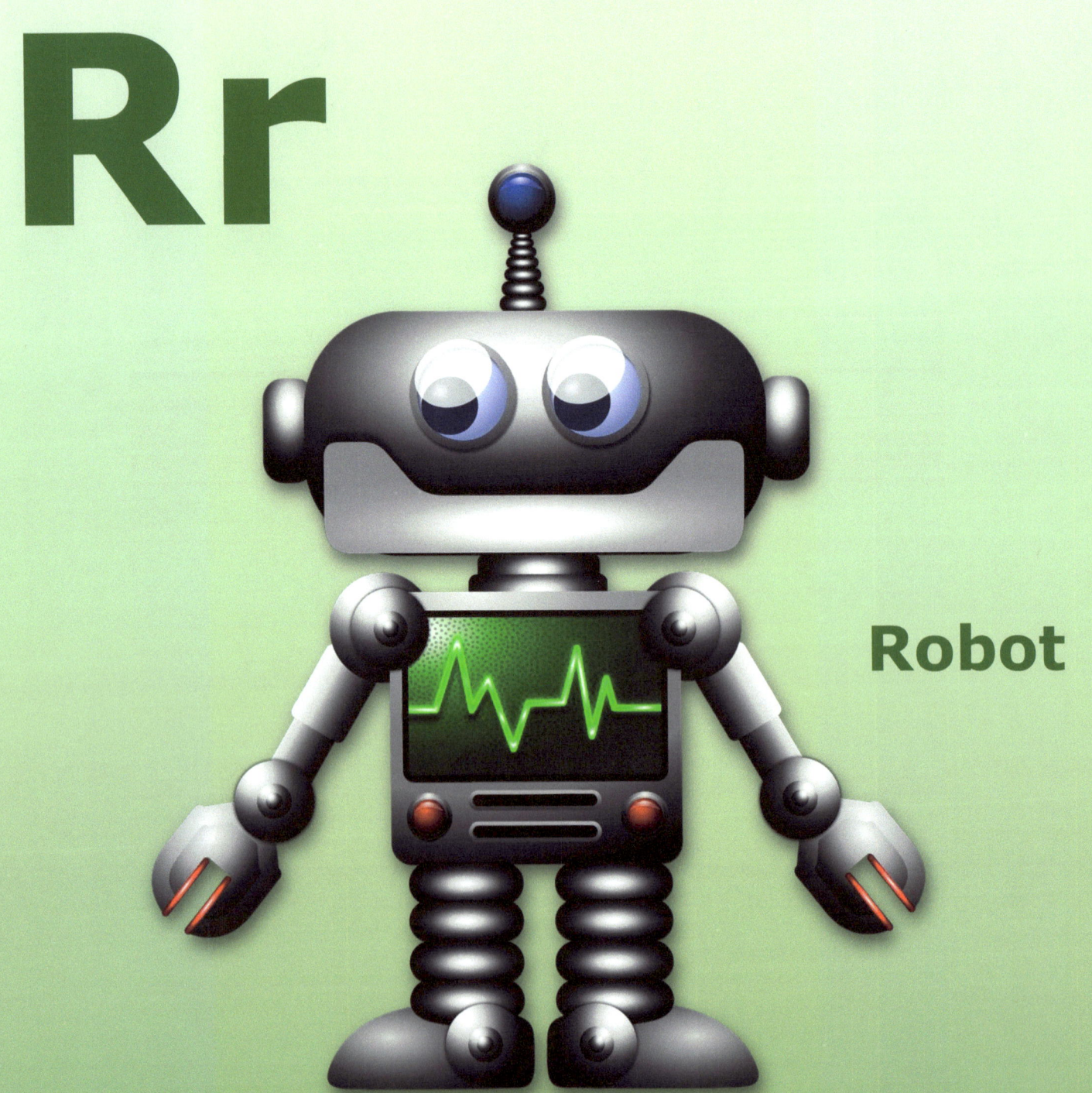

Robot

Ss

Sun

Tt

Turtle

Whale

W w

Xx

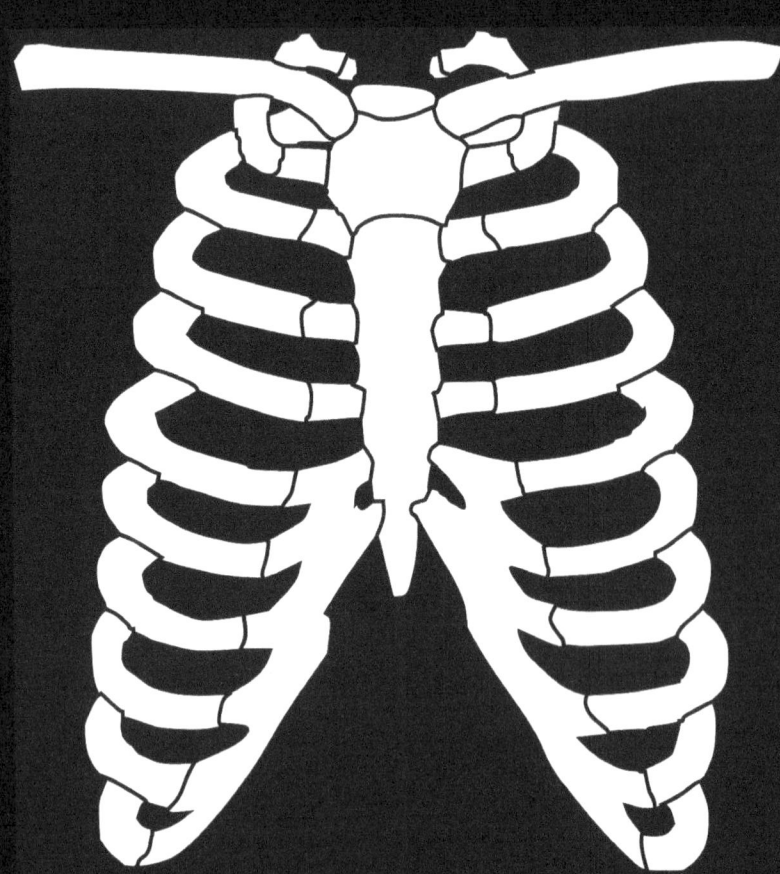

X-ray

Yy

Yellow

www.ingramcontent.com/pod-product-compliance
Lightning Source LLC
Chambersburg PA
CBHW040021050426
42452CB00002B/79